Lungs

Injury, Illness and Health

Carol Ballard

Heinemann Library
Chicago, Illinois

Originated by Ambassador Litho
Printed and bound in Hong Kong, China by South China Printing Company

07 06 05 04 03
10 9 8 7 6 5 4 3 2 1

Library of Congress Cataloging-in-Publication Data
Ballard, Carol
    Lungs / Carol Ballard
        v. cm. -- (Body focus)
Includes bibliographical references and index.
Contents: The respiratory system -- Why do we need oxygen? -- Mouth and nose -- Pharynx and larynx -- Trachea and bronchi -- Airway problems -- Lungs -- Blood supply to the lungs -- Chest investigations -- Chest diseases -- Inside the lungs -- Gaseous exchange -- Asthma -- Lungs and air pollution -- Smoking -- Breathing mechanics -- Breathing control -- Artificial breathing and air supplies -- Respiratory noises -- Breathing emergencies.
    ISBN 1-4034-0198-5 (lib. bdg.) -- ISBN 1-4034-0454-2 (pbk.)
    1. Lungs--Juvenile literature. 2. Respiration--Juvenile literature.
[1. Lungs. 2. Respiratory system.] I. Title. II. Series.
    QP121 .B225 2003
    612.2--dc21

                                                           2002014430

Acknowledgments
The publishers would like to thank the following for permission to reproduce photographs: pp. 4, 9, 23 Science Photo Library; p. 7 Corbis Stockmarket; p. 11Reuters/Steve Marcus; p. 13 Science Photo Library/David M. Martin, M.D.; p. 14 Science Photo Library/Matt Meadows/Peter Arnold; p. 15 Corbis Royalty Free; p. 16 Wellcome Trust; p. 17 Science Photo Library/CNRI; p. 18 Getty Images/Eyewire; p. 21 Science Photo Library/Professor P. Motts/G. Macchiarelli University "Las Sapienza" Rome; p. 22 (top) Science Photo Library/Gusto; p. 22 (bottom) Science Photo Library/John Greim; p. 24 Science Photo Library/Dr. Kari Lounatmaa; p. 25 Science Photo Library/Simon Fraser; p. 27 Science Photo Library/Professor S. Cinti/CNRI; p. 29 Science Photo Library/CNRI; p. 31 Science Photo Library/SBIP/Laurent/B. Hop Ame; p. 32 Science Photo Library/Cape Grim B.A.P.S/Simon Fraser; p. 33 Science Photo Library/Perlstein/Jerrican; p. 34 (left) Science Photo Library/Astrid & Hanns-Frieder Michler; p. 34 (right) Science Photo Library/Manfred Kage; p. 35 Science Photo Library/Custom Medical Stock Photo; p. 38 Corbis/Dat's Jazz; p. 40 Corbis/Roger Ressmeyer; p. 43 Science Photo Library/Geoff Tompkinson.

Cover photograph of a colored X-ray of the lungs of a healthy person reproduced with permission of Science Photo Library.

The publishers would like to thank David Wright for his assistance with the preparation of this book.

Every effort has been made to contact copyright holders of any material reproduced in this book. Any omissions will be rectified in subsequent printings if notice is given to the publishers.

Some words are shown in bold, **like this.** You can find out what they mean by looking in the glossary.

CONTENTS

We need a constant supply of oxygen to stay alive. The respiratory system allows us to obtain oxygen from the air and to get rid of waste carbon dioxide. It also enables us to speak and make other noises, and to do things such as blow up balloons and play wind instruments. The lungs are the main organs involved in the processes of breathing—**inhaling** and **exhaling.** The **diaphragm,** rib cage, and chest muscles are also important in the mechanism of breathing.

Inhaling and exhaling

When we inhale, air enters the body through the nose or mouth and passes into the top of the throat. This leads to the trachea, or windpipe, a tube that branches into two smaller tubes called **bronchi.** The bronchi lead into the lungs, where the blood collects oxygen and releases carbon dioxide. When we exhale, air leaves the body by this same route, but in reverse. As air passes through the voice box, or larynx, the vocal cords move, and these movements make sounds. We control the volume and pitch of the sounds to talk, shout, and sing.

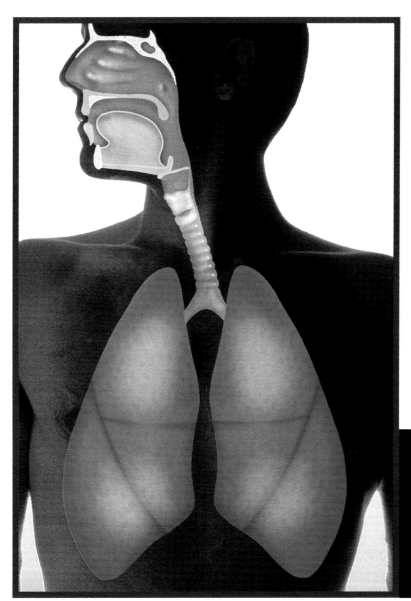

This artwork of the lungs and respiratory system has been placed over a photograph of a man's torso. It shows how air is breathed in through the nose and mouth and travels down the trachea into the two lungs.

The ribs form a bony cage around the lungs, protecting them from injury. Together with associated muscles, the flexible rib cage helps the lungs to expand and contract as we breathe in and out. The diaphragm is a strong, domed sheet of muscle and connective tissue that forms a complete wall between the bottom of the chest and the top of the abdomen. It plays an important role in the body's breathing process.

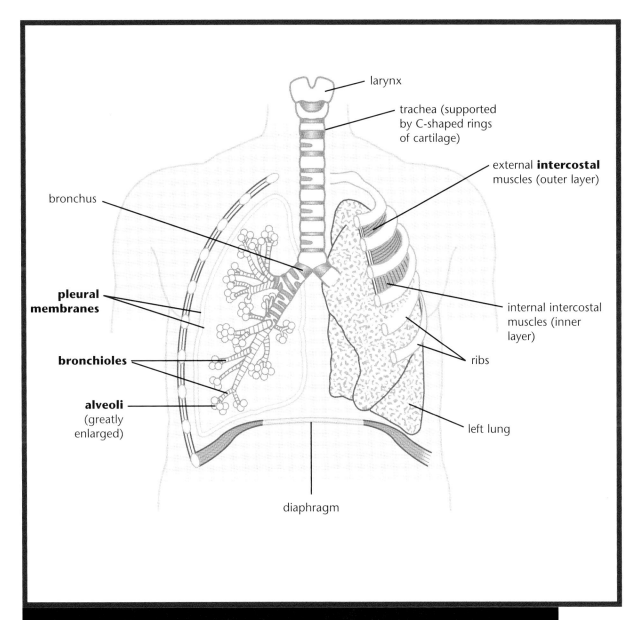

larynx

trachea (supported by C-shaped rings of cartilage)

external **intercostal** muscles (outer layer)

bronchus

pleural membranes

internal intercostal muscles (inner layer)

bronchioles

ribs

alveoli (greatly enlarged)

left lung

diaphragm

This picture shows the structures that make up the respiratory system. It also shows the rib cage and diaphragm—these are not parts of the respiratory system, but they are essential in making the chest movements that enable us to breathe.

WHY DO WE NEED OXYGEN?

With the exception of some **microorganisms,** every living thing needs oxygen in order to survive. It plays a key role in **aerobic respiration** (also called cellular respiration), a process that releases stored energy.

When we eat, our food is broken down into smaller and smaller pieces, until eventually it is separated into individual **molecules** that our bodies can use. These molecules are absorbed into the bloodstream and transported to every part of the body. One of these molecules is glucose, a **carbohydrate.** Foods that contain a lot of glucose include cookies, cakes, pasta, bread, and rice. Other foods contain molecules that can be converted into glucose.

Aerobic respiration

When glucose reaches individual cells, the process of aerobic respiration can take place. This is a complicated chain of chemical changes, and each step needs its own special enzyme to help it to happen. An enzyme is a **protein** that speeds up a **chemical reaction** but does not get used up itself. Enzymes split glucose molecules into even smaller molecules. Oxygen joins with some of the molecules to make water and carbon dioxide, and the energy stored in the glucose molecule is released.

This can be summarized as an equation:

$$\text{glucose} + \text{oxygen} \longrightarrow \text{water} + \text{carbon dioxide} + \text{energy}$$
$$(C_6H_{12}O_6 + 6O_2 \longrightarrow 6H_2O + 6CO_2 + \text{energy})$$

The water made during aerobic respiration is absorbed by the body tissues. Excess water is transported in the bloodstream to the kidneys, then leaves the body as urine. The carbon dioxide made during aerobic respiration is carried by the blood to the lungs, where it leaves the body when we breathe out.

The process of aerobic respiration is **exothermic,** with some of the released energy appearing as heat that is used to maintain our correct body temperature. The rest of the released energy is used to make a chemical called adenosine triphosphate, or ATP. The body's cells store ATP and can use its energy when they need it, to drive other chemical reactions. Some of these reactions just happen inside the cells without our noticing, but they are essential for keeping our bodies functioning normally. We are aware of the results of other reactions—such as those that make muscles contract and relax, allowing us to move.

When we work hard, our muscles need more energy. We breathe faster to get enough oxygen to release the energy we need.

Respiration and exercise

When we exercise vigorously, our muscles need more energy, so aerobic respiration has to be speeded up to release it. The harder we work, the more oxygen we need, so the faster we have to breathe. If we exercise too vigorously, our muscles are not able to get enough oxygen. They can release energy by another process—**anaerobic respiration**—that does not need oxygen. During this process, glucose is broken down into lactic acid, and energy is released.

$$\text{glucose} \longrightarrow \text{lactic acid} + \text{energy}$$
$$(C_6H_{12}O_6 \longrightarrow 2C_3H_6O_3 + \text{energy})$$

However, less energy is released than in aerobic respiration. Also, lactic acid is poisonous and must be broken down quickly into carbon dioxide and water—and this change needs oxygen.

$$\text{lactic acid} + \text{oxygen} \longrightarrow \text{carbon dioxide} + \text{water}$$
$$(2C_3H_6O_3 + 6O_2 \longrightarrow 6CO_2 + 6H_2O)$$

If too much lactic acid builds up in the muscles, they ache and you may get cramps. The build-up of lactic acid is said to create an "oxygen debt." This means that after exercise involving anaerobic respiration, extra oxygen is needed to break down the lactic acid and bring everything back to normal.

Air enters and leaves the body through the mouth and nose. As air passes through the **nasal cavity,** it is cleaned, warmed, and moistened. We can smell chemicals in the air as it passes through our nose and stimulates **sensory** cells.

The part of our face that we call our nose is made of plates of **cartilage** attached to the nasal bone of the skull. Cartilage is strong, giving the nose its shape, but it is also flexible, allowing the nose to bend. A piece of cartilage forms a central wall, making the two nostrils.

Inside the nose

When air enters the nose, it first passes through the vestibule, the space immediately inside each nostril. This is lined by skin with coarse hairs that act as a filter, trapping particles of dust and dirt. The nostrils open into a chamber called the nasal cavity, the space below the base of the skull bone and above the roof of the mouth. The nasal cavity is lined with a special **membrane** called the nasal mucosa. This produces **mucus** to keep all the surfaces moist. Dust particles and **microorganisms** that get past the hairs in the vestibule get trapped in the sticky mucus. The nasal mucosa also contains many tiny **capillaries.** As the blood flows through these, it warms the air.

At the top of the nasal cavity are two small areas, each about the size of a thumbnail, called the olfactory centers. These contain millions of olfactory cells. Long hairs called **cilia** stick out from these cells into the mucus layer. When chemicals in the air travel past them, they respond. The olfactory cells send electrical signals along the olfactory nerves to the brain. The brain interprets the signals, and we "smell" the chemical.

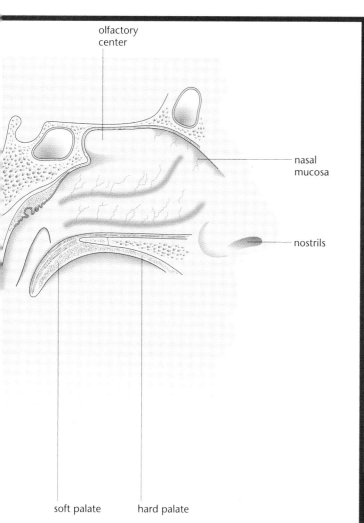

olfactory center

nasal mucosa

nostrils

soft palate

hard palate

This picture shows the structures inside the nasal cavity.

Having a cold

When we have a bad cold, our sense of smell is often dulled. This is because the extra mucus in the nasal cavity prevents air from circulating freely and stimulating the cilia. Blowing the nose and sneezing can help to remove excess mucus. Because the senses of taste and smell are closely linked, the flavors of our food often seem less strong when we have a cold.

Crying

The tear ducts from the eyes drain into the nasal cavity. Normally, the fluid just drains away, but when we cry, we produce too much

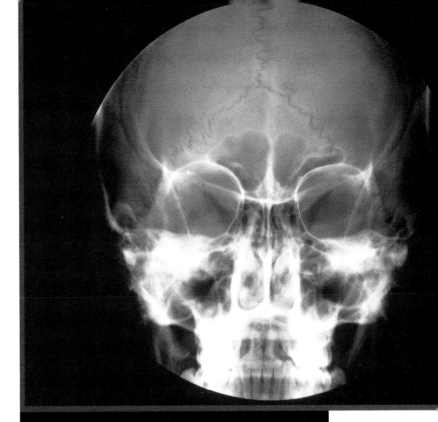

In this X-ray, the skull bones show up as solid white. The sinuses are the dark areas.

fluid for this to happen. Some tears spill over and roll down our faces, but some drain into the nasal cavity, overloading it. That is why you usually need to blow your nose when you have been crying.

Sinuses

The skull also has air spaces called **sinuses.** These are linked to the nasal cavity and are lined with mucous membranes. They are important when we talk or sing because they help make sounds fuller and richer.

Decongestants and sports

If the membranes of the sinuses become inflamed because of an infection or **allergic reaction,** they swell. This can block the openings into the nasal cavity and keep mucus from draining away. As mucus builds up in the sinuses, we suffer a sinus headache. **Decongestant** drugs can be taken to help to clear the sinuses. Many of these can be bought without a doctor's prescription, but anybody taking part in sporting events should be very careful—some of these drugs contain substances that are banned in competitions.

PHARYNX AND LARYNX

After passing through the **nasal cavity,** air moves into the pharynx, the area at the back of the mouth and the top of the throat. The larynx, or voice box, is at the lower part of the pharynx.

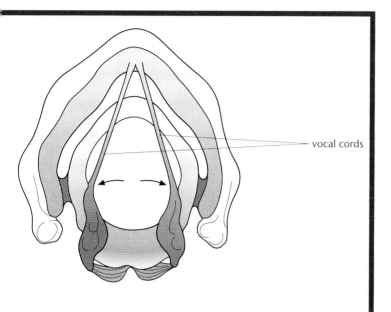

vocal cords

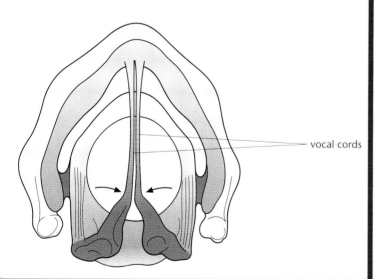

vocal cords

These diagrams sshow the vocal cords and trachea as seen from above. When there is a space between the vocal cords (top), they do not vibrate as air rushes past them, and no sound is made. When the vocal cords are touching (bottom), air passing them will make them vibrate—producing a sound.

The pharynx is a funnel-shaped tube about five inches (thirteen centimeters) long. Its wall is made of muscle, arranged in an outer circular layer made up of rings of muscle and an inner longitudinal layer made up of columns of muscle. It is lined with a moist mucous **membrane.** The pharynx has three main parts:

1. The upper part of the pharynx lies behind the soft palate. When food is swallowed, the flexible soft palate moves up to block off the entrance to this part of the pharynx.

2. The middle part of the pharynx carries air from the nasal cavity and mouth to the trachea, and food from the mouth to the esophagus. When food is swallowed, a flap of elastic **cartilage**—the epiglottis—moves downward to block off the entrance to the trachea. It moves upward again to allow air to enter the trachea. The tonsils form a broken ring around the entrances to the esophagus and trachea. They help to fight infections by destroying foreign substances before they can enter the body.

3. The lower part of the pharynx connects with the trachea and esophagus. It is lined with a mucous membrane to keep it moist, and it has **cilia** to trap dust and other particles.

Adam's apple

The larynx is at the bottom of the pharynx. The walls of the larynx are made of nine pieces of stiff, curved cartilage. The thyroid cartilage, or Adam's apple, is the largest and can be seen beneath the skin at the front of the neck. It is larger in men than in women because male **hormones** stimulate its growth during puberty, but female hormones do not. These pieces of cartilage provide a framework for the vocal cords, two thin shelflike folds of tough tissue that are stretched across the larynx from front to back.

Vocal cords

If we are just breathing normally, there is space between the vocal cords, so there is no noise. When we want to make a sound, muscles in the neck alter the position of the cartilage frame, stretching the vocal cords and moving them toward each other. As air rushes past them, they vibrate, making a noise. Because of the angle of the vocal cords as we **exhale**, it is easier to produce a sound when we are breathing out than when we are breathing in. The tighter the vocal cords are stretched, the faster they vibrate and the higher the sound they produce. Because women's vocal cords are usually shorter and thinner than men's, their voices sound higher.

On stage, a singer must have great control over the larynx, to allow production of exactly the right sounds.

After passing through the larynx, air moves into the trachea. This branches into two narrower tubes, the primary bronchi. These branch again to form the secondary bronchi, and then again and again, eventually ending with the narrowest tubes, the **bronchioles.**

The trachea is a tube that is 4 to 5 inches (12 to 13 centimeters) long and 1 inch (2.5 centimeters) in diameter. It is surrounded by a column of C-shaped rings of **cartilage** that give it support and keep it from collapsing. The rings are connected by stretchy fibers and muscles, so the trachea can bend and stretch as we move. The inside of the trachea is lined with a mucous **membrane** that produces **mucus** to keep the trachea lubricated and moist. It also has **cilia** that help to trap and remove any dust particles or **microorganisms** that enter it.

The trachea's main branches are the right primary **bronchus,** leading into the right lung, and the left primary bronchus, leading into the left lung. These primary bronchi are also supported by rings of cartilage and are lubricated by mucus.

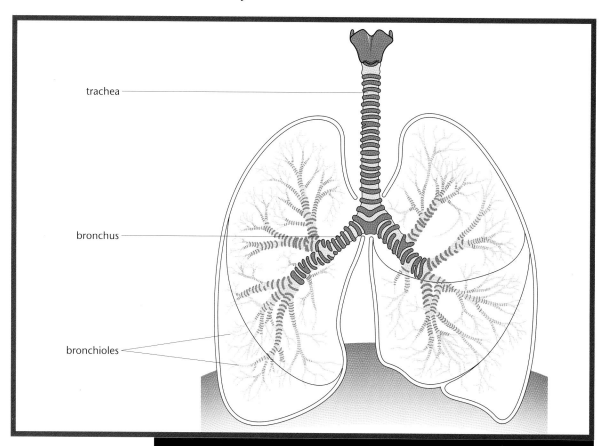

In this picture, you can see how the trachea branches into two bronchi, and they in turn eventually branch into bronchioles.

At the point where the trachea splits is a small ridge called the carina. The mucous membrane here is very sensitive and is the most likely area of the trachea to trigger a cough when stimulated by foreign material, such as dust.

Into the lungs

The lungs are divided into smaller sections called lobes. There is one secondary bronchus for each lobe of each lung—two for the left lung and three for the right. (The left lung is slightly smaller, to make room for the heart.) These branch again into even smaller tertiary bronchi, and then into smaller and smaller bronchioles. As this branching continues, with the

An endoscope allows doctors to see the linings of the airways. This picture shows the vocal cords in the larynx.

passages becoming narrower and narrower, the cartilage rings disappear and the amount of muscle in the walls of the tubes increases. Eventually, the branching ends with the narrowest tubes of all, the terminal bronchioles.

If you look at the system of the trachea, bronchi, and bronchioles upside down, the branching pattern looks sort of like a tree—so these structures are sometimes called the "bronchial tree."

Emergency!

The trachea may be blocked as the result of a chest injury, inflammation, or swallowed object. This situation needs emergency treatment to enable the patient to breathe.

If the blockage is above the larynx, doctors may carry out a tracheotomy, in which a small cut is made in the neck below the larynx. A tube is then inserted, allowing the patient to breathe, as air can enter and leave the lungs via this tube.

Alternatively, a tube can be inserted through the mouth or nose and pushed down through the larynx and trachea. The tube pushes obstructions out of the way and sucks out any excess mucus, allowing the patient to breathe normally again. This procedure is called intubation.

A rush of air through the respiratory system can result in several different noises being made. Some of these we can control, but some are completely uncontrollable!

Sneezing forces air, mucus, dust, and microorganisms out of the nose at high speed.

Sneeze

A sneeze is a sudden involuntary **exhalation** of air through the nose, usually in response to excess **mucus** or dust particles in the **nasal cavity**. Air is forced out at up to 100 miles per hour (160 kilometers per hour)—even greater than the force of a hurricane!

When we sneeze, we **inhale**, and then the back of the tongue blocks the airway to trap the air. Abdominal muscles contract, increasing the pressure inside the chest space. This pressure then forces the air out through the nose. Mucus, dust, and **microorganisms** are carried out too, and may travel as much as ten feet (three meters). Using a tissue or handkerchief to trap our own mucus and germs from a sneeze prevents them from spreading through the air for other people to breathe in.

Cough

Like a sneeze, a cough is a sudden involuntary exhalation of air, but through the mouth instead of the nose. We usually cough in an attempt to dislodge excess mucus, dust particles, or other foreign objects from the airways.

When we cough, we inhale, and muscles in the pharynx and larynx contract to trap the air. Pressure inside the chest increases as the abdominal muscles contract. The pharynx and larynx muscles relax, the airways open, and air is forced out. As the air passes through the larynx, the vocal cords vibrate and make a noise. Mucus is ejected from the airways and is usually swallowed or removed by spitting (again, try to catch your own germs with a handkerchief or tissue).

Hiccup

Nearly everybody has experienced hiccups at some time, so most people know just how uncontrollable they are! Hiccups are the result of sudden short contractions of the **diaphragm.** Air is sucked in so quickly that the epiglottis snaps shut noisily.

Sometimes hiccups occur when the stomach is very full, because it irritates the diaphragm and nerves above it. Sometimes they occur for no apparent reason.

An attack of hiccups is usually over in a few minutes. Sometimes holding your breath for a short time can help to stop hiccups by forcing the diaphragm to remain still.

Yawning is a way to quickly take oxygen into the lungs after exhaling, but it can also be a sign of boredom!

Snore

Snoring occurs when the throat muscles are relaxed and the upper airway is partly blocked by the soft palate and the uvula (a flap of soft tissue that hangs down from the soft palate). As the person breathes in and out, the soft palate and the uvula vibrate noisily as air passes over them.

Snoring is often worse when people sleep on their backs, so sleeping on one side or changing the angle of the head can often reduce it. Nasal **decongestants** can sometimes help, too. Some people may also get relief using variety of clips and pegs that are available for the nose.

Yawn

There are several things that may cause us to yawn, but it is not clear whether one is more important than the others. We often yawn when we are tired, bored, or sitting in a stuffy room.

If we are being still and quiet, our breathing rate may slow down so much that not enough carbon dioxide is released. Yawning rapidly clears any excess carbon dioxide out of the lungs. If our breathing rate is slow, or the atmosphere is stuffy, we may not be taking in enough oxygen. Yawning rapidly fills the lungs with a fresh supply of oxygen.

When we yawn, many muscles of the face contract and then relax. This may stimulate the blood supply to the head, including the brain, and help us to feel more alert again.

The pharynx, larynx, trachea, and **bronchi** can all be affected by **bacteria** and **viruses,** and they can be irritated by dust and smoke. In an acute infection, problems may develop quickly, but in a chronic infection they may come on slowly and last for months or years.

Pharyngitis

Pharyngitis, an inflammation of the pharynx, usually results in a sore throat. Acute pharyngitis is often the first sign of a viral infection such as the common cold or **influenza.** The *Streptococcus* bacterium can also cause a sore throat, usually known as "strep throat." Infections from other nearby sites, such as the tonsils and **sinuses,** can also affect the pharynx. Chronic pharyngitis is often caused by smoking and drinking too much alcohol.

Antibiotics can quickly clear up a bacterial infection, but have no effect on a viral infection or on chronic pharyngitis. Comfort remedies, such as warm drinks and throat lozenges, can help to ease the soreness.

Laryngitis

Laryngitis is an inflammation of the larynx. Acute laryngitis is usually caused by an infection, such as influenza or a common cold, or by the strain of shouting or singing. Irritation of the larynx by cigarette smoke can also lead to laryngitis. Chronic laryngitis is most commonly the result of irritation by breathing tobacco smoke or dust, or by using the voice too much over a long period. Laryngitis is usually cured by resting the voice for a few days. Inhaling warm steam can often help, too.

Polyps and nodes

Polyps are tiny lumps that can develop on the vocal cords, making the voice sound hoarse and breathy. Vocal cord nodes are also tiny lumps, developing from long-term overuse of the voice. For example, many teachers who have raised their voices in the classroom for years suffer from these. Both polyps and nodes can be surgically removed.

This photograph shows a polyp on the larynx.

Tonsillitis

Tonsillitis is an inflammation of the tonsils, usually caused by *Streptococcus* bacteria. The tonsils swell and produce pus, the throat feels uncomfortable, and it is hard to swallow. Some patients also suffer from earaches and stiff necks if the tubes that connect the ear and throat become blocked.

Tonsillitis is most common in young children and during puberty. This may be because the tonsils grow during childhood, but then begin to shrink at puberty. Pain can be relieved with warm drinks, and antibiotics can cure bacterial infections. If a child suffers repeated infections, doctors may decide that the tonsils should be surgically removed.

Bronchitis

The main cause of chronic bronchitis is cigarette smoke, which irritates the lining of the bronchi. They then produce a lot of sticky **mucus** blocking the airways and keeping the **cilia** from working normally. Any **microorganisms** that reach the bronchi are therefore not removed, and they can multiply, causing infection.

Bronchitis is marked by a persistent cough, often with wheezing and shortness of breath. Patients with bronchitis find it difficult to exercise or play sports, and sometimes just walking up stairs or moving around a room is difficult. Treatments include breathing exercises and oxygen therapy, a system that increases a patient's oxygen intake by supplying pure oxygen through a face mask.

Emphysema

In a case of emphysema, the tiny air sacs called **alveoli** get permanently stretched and filled with air, so the lungs are less elastic. People with emphysema find any kind of exertion difficult and are always breathless. Daily activities can cause attacks of breathlessness, followed by coughing. Emphysema cannot be cured, but oxygen treatment can help, and some drugs can clear the airways.

In this picture, taken using an endoscope, you can see the cilia that keep the airways clear of dust and microorganisms.

The lungs are inside the chest, protected by the rib cage. They are pinkish-gray, spongy organs, roughly cone-shaped, with a narrow tip and a wide base. They are surrounded by **membranes** containing fluid that lubricates them, allowing them to move freely during breathing.

Lung protection

The lungs are protected by a bony cage made by twelve pairs of ribs, together with the **sternum** and the thoracic **vertebrae,** which form the upper backbone. The first ten pairs of ribs are connected to the sternum by flexible strips of **cartilage,** allowing them to move. The bottom two pairs of ribs are "floating ribs" and are only connected to the vertebrae. The ribs are moved when the muscles they are connected to contract and relax, increasing and then decreasing the space inside the rib cage during the process of breathing in and out.

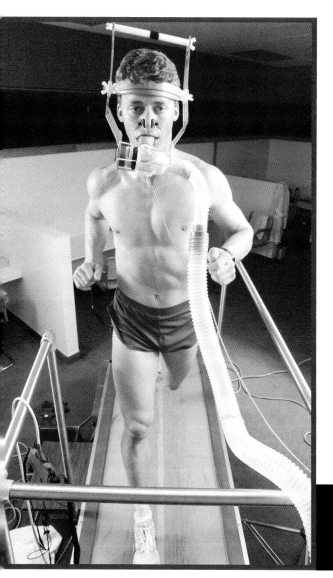

Inside the lungs

The lungs fill most of the space inside the chest. Each lung is enclosed and protected by a **pleural membrane** with two layers. There is a space between the layers called the pleural cavity. This space contains a liquid the membranes produce, known as pleural fluid. This fluid reduces friction between the membranes so they can slide easily over each other when we breathe. The pleural membranes may become inflamed, causing an illness called pleurisy.

The narrow tip of each lung is called the apex. The wide base of each lung is arched to fit over the dome-shaped **diaphragm.** The right lung has three lobes—upper (superior), middle, and lower (inferior). The left lung is slightly smaller than the right lung because it has a small hollow where the heart lies. This lung has only two lobes—superior and inferior.

This athlete is using a spirometer to measure his lung capacity. It will record how much air he breathes in and out as he runs on the treadmill.

The left and right lung are joined in the center by an area called the hilus, or root. This is where **bronchi,** major blood vessels, lymphatic vessels (which allow drainage of excess fluid), and nerves enter and exit each lung.

The amount of air the lungs can hold is called the **lung capacity.** It can be measured using a spirometer or respirometer and recorded on a chart recorder or monitor.

Lung capacity

The lungs of a healthy adult man can hold about 6.3 quarts (6 liters) of air. The average woman's lung capacity is slightly lower than a man's.

- When resting, an adult usually breathes in and out about ten to fifteen times every minute. With each breath, about 1 pint (0.5 liters) of air enters and leaves the lungs. This is the "tidal volume."
- There is always some air left in the lungs. This "residual volume" is usually about 1.3 quarts (1.2 liters).
- The maximum amount of air that can be breathed out after taking the deepest possible breath is about 3.7–4.8 quarts (3.5–4.5 liters) and is called the "vital capacity."
- The maximum amount of air that the lungs can hold is about 6.3 quarts (6 liters). This is the lung capacity.

In normal breathing, we use only a small fraction of our full lung capacity. When we exercise, we need to increase the amount of air we breathe in and out. You can do this by breathing more quickly, or by breathing more deeply. When you breathe normally, about 0.15 quarts (0.15 liters) of air stays in the nasal passages, trachea, bronchi, and **bronchioles,** so it cannot be used by the body.

This table shows why slow, deep breathing is much more efficient than fast, shallow breathing.

	Fast and shallow 50 breaths / min.	Even and regular 20 breaths / min.	Slow and deep 10 breaths / min.
Air in with each breath	0.2 quarts	0.5 quarts	1 quart
Total air in	50 x 0.2 = 10 quarts	20 x 0.5 = 10 quarts	10 x 1 = 10 quarts
Air not reaching lungs	50 x 0.15 = 7.5 quarts	20 x 0.15 = 3 quarts	10 x 0.15 = 1.5 quarts
Air reaching lungs	10 – 7.5 = 2.5 quarts	10 – 3 = 7 quarts	10 – 1.5 = 8.5 quarts

BLOOD SUPPLY TO THE LUNGS

Each lung needs a good supply of blood to allow collection of oxygen and elimination of carbon dioxide. This is provided by major blood vessels carrying blood directly to the lungs from the heart.

The circulation of blood from the heart to the lungs and back to the heart is a separate loop from the rest of the body's blood supply. It is called the **pulmonary** circulation. In this loop, the heart pumps **deoxygenated** blood to the lungs, and **oxygenated** blood flows back to the heart. In addition, the bronchial arteries supply oxygenated blood to the tissues of the lungs themselves, and deoxygenated blood is removed through the bronchial veins. This is part of the main circulatory loop of the body.

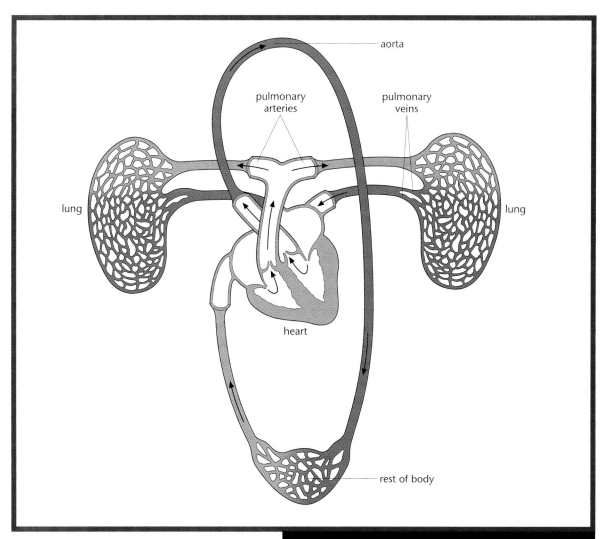

This diagram shows how the lungs are linked to the heart and major blood vessels. The area labeled "rest of body" is not shown to scale.

Pulmonary circulation

Deoxygenated blood leaves the right side of the heart through the pulmonary trunk. This is very short, branching almost immediately into two: the right pulmonary artery takes blood to the right lung, and the left pulmonary artery takes blood to the left lung. The pulmonary arteries are the only arteries in the body that carry deoxygenated blood.

Inside each lung, the pulmonary arteries branch into smaller vessels, carrying blood to each lobe. These vessels branch again and again, eventually forming the very narrowest vessels, the **capillaries.** These have very thin walls to allow gases and other substances to move between the blood and body tissues by a process known as diffusion. This means that **molecules** of a particular gas or chemical move from a place where the concentration is high to a place where the concentration is lower, balancing the concentration. As blood passes through the capillaries, it loses carbon dioxide and collects oxygen.

This photograph shows the capillaries surrounding the **alveoli** inside the lungs.

Capillaries unite to form larger vessels, and these rejoin to form the right pulmonary vein in the right lung and the left pulmonary vein in the left lung. These large vessels carry freshly oxygenated blood back to the left side of the heart, from where it is pumped around to the rest of the body. This complete pulmonary circulation, from heart to lungs and back to the heart, takes only four to eight seconds.

Blockage

A blockage in any part of the pulmonary circulation can be very serious. A blood clot, air bubble, or piece of debris can be carried around the body in large blood vessels, eventually reaching the heart. If something like this is pumped out of the heart and into the pulmonary circulation, it can become lodged in one of the smaller vessels inside the lungs and block the blood flow through the lung. This blockage is called a pulmonary embolism. A serious blockage can cause a patient to collapse, requiring vital emergency treatment. However, even with good medical care, the patient may still die.

Most pulmonary embolisms are caused by blood clots, and are treated by drugs to make the clot dissolve. Other drugs, such as aspirin, can make the blood less sticky, reducing the risk of more clots forming in the future.

CHEST INVESTIGATIONS

The lungs are vital organs, so it is important that they are working properly. Doctors can examine the lungs using a variety of techniques to determine what problems may be present and to decide on the best course of treatment.

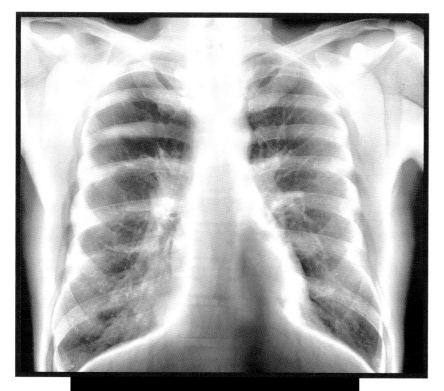

Chest X-ray

An X-ray gives information about the lung tissue. Diseased lung tissue blocks the path of X-rays more than healthy lung tissue does, so it shows up as a shadow (a white patch) on the X-ray. Shadows are usually seen as the result of infections (such as tuberculosis) or other diseases (such as lung cancer). Fluid build-up can also be detected by X-rays, indicating the possibility of a disease such as pleurisy.

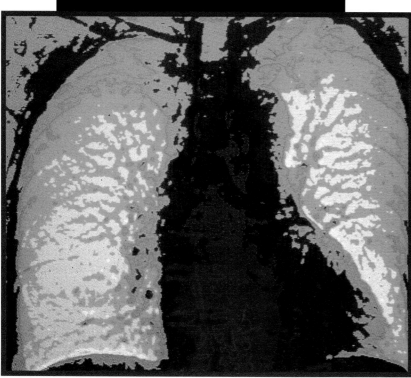

Different types of scans give different information. The first picture (top left) shows a chest X-ray, and the ribs show up more clearly than the lungs themselves. The second picture (left) is a CAT scan, showing a lot more detailed information than that provided by the X-ray.

CAT scan

If doctors need more detailed information than an ordinary X-ray can provide, a CAT (computerized axial tomography) scan can be used. This shows the blood vessels and the airways inside the lungs, in a series of "slices" through the chest. The images produced allow doctors to pinpoint the precise location and extent of disease. A CAT scan is about 100 times more sensitive than an ordinary X-ray.

For a CAT scan, patients lie still inside a scanner that is like a large metal tube. The scan takes about twenty minutes, as the scanner is rotated a full 360° around the patient's body.

The scanner passes an X-ray beam through the body. A detector picks it up and sends the information into a computer for analysis. An image is shown on a monitor, with the most dense material showing up as white, less dense material as shades of gray, and liquid and air as black. For extra clarity, colors may be used instead of just gray shades.

Bronchoscopy

During a bronchoscopy, a flexible tube containing hundreds of glass fibers is inserted into the patient's trachea through the nose or mouth. When light shines on the glass fibers, they act like a tubular mirror and reflect the image up to the eyepiece. This gives the doctor a clear picture of the inside surfaces of the airways. The bronchoscope can be maneuvered around inside the main **bronchi** and can even be used to take samples. It is useful for examining only the bigger airways, as it is too large to enter the narrower passages.

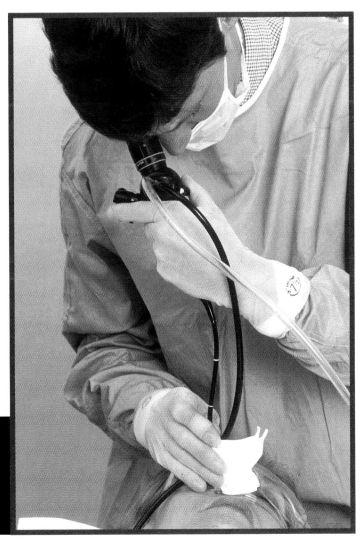

This asthma patient is being examined using a bronchoscope. The doctor will be able to take samples from her airways to examine under a microscope.

LUNG DISEASES

Pleurisy

Pleurisy is an infection of the **pleural membranes,** usually caused by **microorganisms** that may enter the body through the airways during normal breathing. As the patient breathes in and out, the pleural membranes rub against each other rather than sliding smoothly as they do in a healthy lung. This rubbing makes a scratchy, grating sound and causes intense pain. Sometimes, watery liquid or pus builds up in the pleural cavity and can be seen on an X-ray.

Treatment usually includes **antibiotics** to kill the microorganisms responsible for the infection and painkillers to help keep the patient comfortable. If a large amount of fluid and pus collects, it may be necessary to remove it. A special, hollow needle is inserted through the chest wall into the pleural cavity, allowing the fluid to drain away.

Pneumonia

Pneumonia is an acute inflammation of the narrowest airways of the lungs. Fluid builds up in these airways, preventing the lungs from functioning normally. In the United States, there are an estimated four million cases every year—most commonly among young children, elderly people, and smokers.

Pneumonia is caused by infection with a microorganism, usually by a **bacterium** called *Streptococcus pneumoniae.* However, other microorganisms that enter the lungs through the airways during normal breathing can also be responsible.

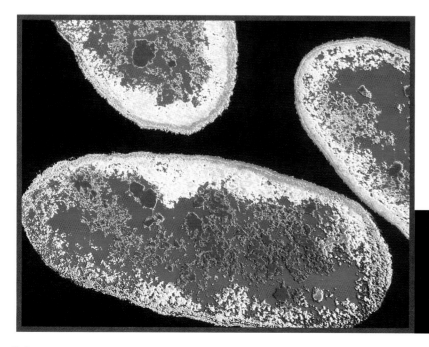

Pneumonia causes fever, chills, coughs, chest pain, and tiredness. Patients are usually treated with antibiotics to kill the microorganisms, drugs to clear the airways, and chest **physiotherapy.**

Aeromonas hydrophila, a bacteria associated with pneumonia, is resistant to many antibiotics, including penicillin.

Tuberculosis (TB)

Tuberculosis (TB) is caused by infection with the microorganism *Mycobacterium tuberculosis.* The bacterium damages lung tissue, making holes in the lung that cannot be repaired. It can be passed on by contact with someone already infected, or by **inhalation** of the bacterium.

Worldwide, it is the most common infectious disease—there are an estimated eight million new cases every year, with three million people dying from it annually. During the twentieth century, tuberculosis has become much less common in developed countries, as housing conditions and diet have improved. Vaccination programs in many countries have also helped to reduce the incidence of the disease, but in many poorer countries, tuberculosis is still very common.

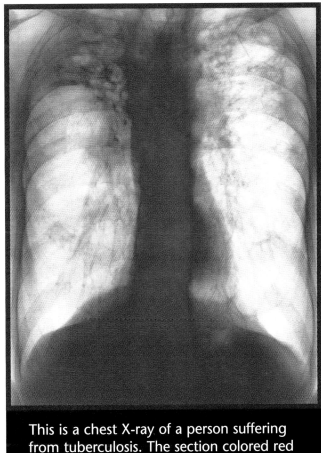

This is a chest X-ray of a person suffering from tuberculosis. The section colored red in one of the lungs is the affected area.

Many people carry the TB bacterium but do not develop the disease. This is called latent TB. In these cases, the body is able to fight the bacteria and keep them from growing. However, the bacteria stay alive in the body, and they can become active later, especially if the immune system weakens. People with latent TB show no symptoms and cannot spread the disease. A simple test can show whether a person has latent TB.

In some cases, if the immune system is not strong enough to fight the TB bacteria, a person will develop TB disease. Symptoms include a persistent cough, chest pain, weakness, fever, and coughing up blood. Most cases of TB can by cured with antibiotics.

Cystic fibrosis

Cystic fibrosis is an inherited disease that affects the lungs and other organs. The lungs produce thick **mucus** that does not drain away easily. As the mucus builds up, the airways become blocked and inflamed, and the patient finds it difficult to breathe. Chest physiotherapy is needed every day to prevent mucus build-up, and antibiotics can help to reduce chest infections.

INSIDE THE LUNGS

The terminal **bronchioles** branch again to form tiny tubes called alveolar ducts. These lead into microscopic hollow balls called **alveoli.** The whole structure looks a bit like a bunch of grapes, with the bronchioles as the stalk and the alveoli as the grapes.

Each lung contains more than 300 million alveoli. Although each is tiny, together they provide a huge internal surface area, many times greater than the surface area of the skin. A single alveolus is only about 0.001 inch (0.025 millimeter) in diameter—it would take about 1,000 to make one inch. The alveolar walls are thicker in some places than others, varying from less than 0.00004 inch (0.001 millimeter) to 0.0004 inch (0.01 millimeter). At their thinnest, they are just a single cell thick, to allow the gases oxygen and carbon dioxide to move between the alveoli and the **capillaries.** Each alveolus is closely surrounded by capillaries that form a meshlike network over its surface.

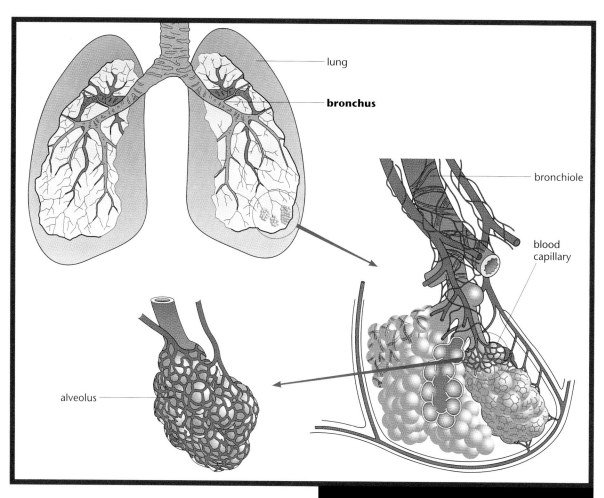

This series of pictures shows the structure of an area of lung, with increasing magnification.

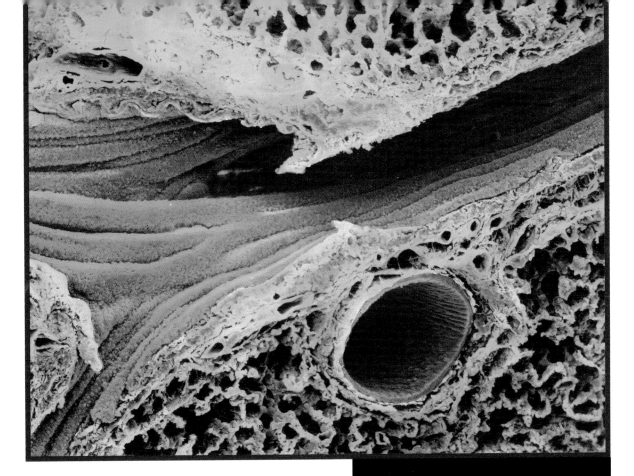

Alveolar fluid

The lining of each alveolus produces alveolar fluid. This fluid keeps the internal walls of the alveoli moist and moistens the incoming air as well. Alveolar fluid also contains lung surfactant, a substance that helps keep the alveoli fully inflated. Lung surfactant works by reducing the surface tension of the water on the inner walls of the alveoli, keeping them from collapsing inward and sticking together.

Babies do not breathe air before birth, so their alveoli are not inflated, and they do not need alveolar fluid. However, they need to breathe as soon as they are born, so the alveoli have to inflate. If there is too little alveolar fluid, the alveoli may not inflate, or may inflate and collapse again, making the baby unable to breathe properly. Premature babies are particularly at risk from this complication and may need to spend some time in an incubator before they can breathe without assistance.

Alveolar walls

The alveolar walls do not have **cilia** to keep them free from debris. Instead, the alveoli contain specialized white blood cells called macrophages. Some stick to the inside of the alveolar wall, and some move around freely inside the alveoli. They surround and destroy **microorganisms** and other foreign particles that enter the alveoli.

GASEOUS EXCHANGE

Breathing in and out is the mechanism that lets the body get rid of waste carbon dioxide and collect fresh oxygen. This swapping of one gas for another takes place in the **alveoli**. The process is called gaseous exchange, and it occurs by diffusion. This means that **molecules** of a gas move from an area of high concentration to one where the concentration is lower, balancing the concentration.

Gaseous exchange is possible only because the walls of the **capillaries** and the walls of the alveoli are very close to each other, and are so thin that gas molecules can pass through them in both directions.

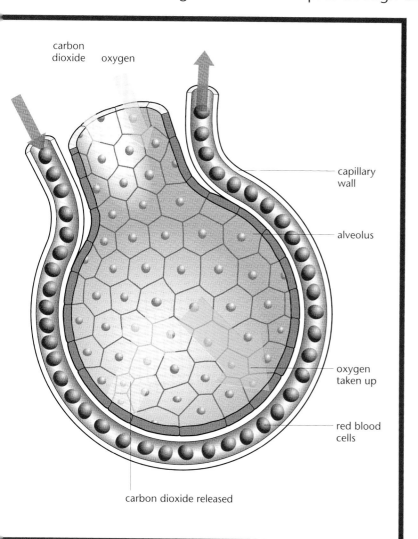

carbon dioxide oxygen

capillary wall

alveolus

oxygen taken up

red blood cells

carbon dioxide released

This diagram shows how gases are exchanged as blood passes through the capillaries in the lungs. Oxygen diffuses out of the alveolus into the blood. Carbon dioxide diffuses in the opposite direction.

When we breathe in, the alveoli fill with air that has a high concentration of oxygen. The blood in the capillaries has a low oxygen concentration. This means that the oxygen levels are unbalanced, and the oxygen in the alveoli moves to even this out. Oxygen molecules spread out and dissolve in the thin layer of fluid that lines the inside of the alveolar walls. They can then move through the alveolar wall, through the capillary wall, and into the blood, where they get picked up by the red blood cells.

At the same time, the blood flowing through the capillaries is rich in carbon dioxide. A tiny amount is carried by red blood cells, but most of it is dissolved in the plasma, the liquid part of the blood. The air in the alveoli contains less carbon dioxide, so the carbon dioxide molecules move out of the blood, through the capillary wall, through the alveolar wall, and into the alveoli. They then leave the alveoli as we exhale.

Capillaries are just large enough for red blood cells to squeeze through, as this photomicrograph shows.

Diffusion

This movement of molecules from a place where the concentration is high to a place where the concentration is low is called diffusion. It happens all the time in the air around us.

If you spray some perfume at one end of a room, the smell will eventually reach a person at the other end of the room. This happens because the perfume molecules move through the air from the place where there is a high concentration (next to the perfume bottle) to the place where there is little (farther across the room). This movement of the molecules continues until they are spread evenly throughout the room.

Oxygen is carried around in the red blood cells by a large molecule called **hemoglobin.** Oxygen joins onto the hemoglobin and can be detached when it is needed elsewhere in the body.

Carbon monoxide poisoning

Another gas, carbon monoxide, can also join on to hemoglobin. When that happens, it prevents oxygen from joining to the hemoglobin—so if carbon monoxide is inhaled, less oxygen can be carried around the body. Eventually, the body cells become so starved for oxygen that the person dies. This is known as carbon monoxide poisoning. Some household appliances, such as gas-powered heaters, can emit carbon monoxide, but special detectors, which alert you if there is too much carbon monoxide in a room, are available. Car exhaust contains carbon monoxide, too, so it is not a good idea to leave a car's engine running in a confined space such as a garage.

Carbon monoxide and oxygen also compete for hemoglobin in people who smoke cigarettes. One-fifth of a smoker's hemoglobin may be bound to carbon monoxide, making it unavailable to transport oxygen around the body.

 ASTHMA

Asthma, a condition that causes breathlessness, coughing, and wheezing, is becoming increasingly common. Doctors think this may be due to a variety of changes in our diets and in our environment. Luckily, asthma can usually be controlled with medication. There are several types of asthma, but in most young people it is an **allergic reaction** that happens when they are exposed to a particular substance.

Causes of asthma

The most common cause of asthma in children and teenagers is an allergy to something in their environment, such as pollen, house dust, pet fur, or air pollution. In patients who develop asthma when they are older, there are probably other triggers, such as medicines or chemicals they handle. Asthma attacks can also be triggered by certain foods, exercise, breathing in hot or cold air, or emotional upsets.

Allergy tests can be carried out to discover whether there is a specific trigger—something **inhaled,** eaten, or touched—that causes a person's asthma attacks. In many cases, once people know what causes their asthma, they are able to avoid it completely, or at least keep their exposure to it to a minimum.

Symptoms

In patients suffering from asthma, the **bronchi** are inflamed. They swell, so they become narrower, restricting the flow of air into and out of the lungs. When muscles in the walls of the airways are irritated, they contract, making the airways even narrower and making breathing more difficult. The inflammation also means that too much sticky **mucus** is produced, which blocks the airways even more.

Treatment

Asthma can be treated with drugs. Many patients have inhalers that they can use to deliver the drugs when they need them. There are two types of inhalers:
- Reliever inhalers can be used to help relieve a specific attack. These are used only when needed.
- Preventer inhalers are used to control the underlying inflammation. They need to be used regularly, even when the patient has no symptoms, to prevent further attacks.

Patients may have either or both of these types of inhalers, depending on the problems they have. As with all medicines, it is important that you take only what has been prescribed for you personally. Somebody else's inhaler may look identical to yours, but it could contain a very different medicine.

Asthma attacks

Severe asthma attacks can require emergency treatment. Bronchodilator drugs need to be given immediately. They relieve the spasm and widen the airways so that the patient can breathe normally again. The most effective way of delivering these drugs is with a nebulizer. This produces a fine mist of the drug dissolved in water, which the patient inhales through a mask or mouthpiece. After a severe attack, a patient may need to take some **steroid** drugs for a while to reduce the inflammation and the risk of another attack.

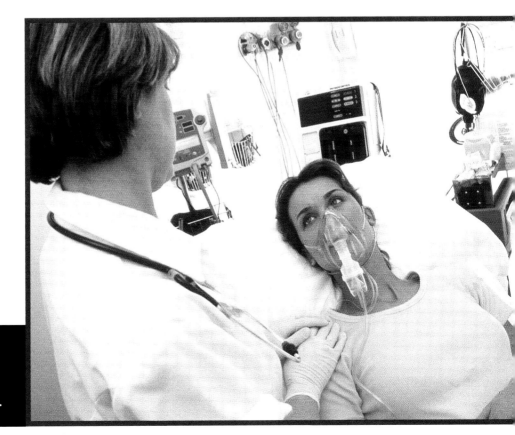

This patient has been given an oxygen mask to help her to breathe.

There are many sources and types of air pollution. Some are found generally in the air around us, and others are found only in restricted areas. Air pollution can cause a variety of breathing difficulties and lung problems. Governments, companies, and individuals are trying to find ways of reducing air pollution and people's exposure to it.

Air pollution levels can be very different in different places, and even in one place at different times. It is often thought of as a modern problem but has been around ever since people began to build factories with smoking chimneys. In the late nineteenth century, an environmental officer in northern England noted that the smoke from chimneys was black with soot particles and was so acidic that it was eating away metal and stone. Stricter laws and the use of smokeless fuels in some places have helped to reduce this kind of problem. However, in recent years, air pollution has become significantly worse in other ways as the use of motor vehicles has increased.

Air pollution can trigger many lung problems. Weather forecasts often contain data about expected pollution levels so that people who are vulnerable, such as the elderly and those who suffer from asthma, can protect themselves accordingly.

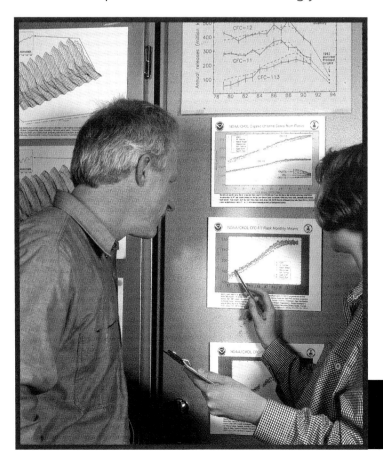

Measures to reduce pollution

As we begin to realize the amount of damage air pollution can do to our health and to the environment, measures are being introduced to reduce it. Cars with catalytic converters break down the harmful carbon monoxide and nitrogen oxide of exhaust fumes to harmless gases, but they still produce some pollutants. Lead-free and low-sulfur gasoline also reduces the pollution. Many industrial chimneys are now fitted with special filters to clean the gases

Scientists collect statistical information to measure air pollution levels.

before they are released into the atmosphere. We have done a lot—but most people would agree that there is still a lot more to do.

Pneumoconiosis

Pneumoconiosis is a general name for a group of diseases resulting from the air pollution that some people are exposed to because of the jobs they do. They are all caused by **inhalation** of different types of dust particles over a long period of time, resulting in inflammation and other damage to the lungs. Healthy tissue is replaced by scar tissue, and in some cases, pneumoconiosis may lead to lung cancer.

In developed countries, people working in conditions where they may be exposed to potentially harmful air pollutants are required to wear protective clothing such as face masks. If the risk is high, such as in demolishing buildings that contain asbestos, workers may need special breathing equipment. In poorer areas, however, such precautions are often not available.

In busy cities, some people try to avoid inhaling polluted air by wearing masks that filter out the pollutants.

Treatment

Treatment of these diseases depends on the extent and seriousness of the lung damage caused. In some cases, drugs and oxygen therapy may help to relieve the symptoms. In others, surgery to remove damaged lung tissue may be appropriate.

Disease	Cause	People affected
asbestosis	asbestos fibers	builders and demolition workers
silicosis	silicon particles	silicon miners
anthracosis	coal dust	coal miners
fibrosing alveolitis, or "farmer's lung"	hay, straw, other farm materials	farmers and others associated with livestock

Cigarette smoke causes serious damage to the lungs and other parts of the body. This can lead to diseases that, in many cases, are fatal. The contents of cigarette smoke are addictive, making it difficult to give it up—so it makes sense not to start in the first place!

The components of cigarette smoke

The lungs of a healthy person are pale and clean. However, the tar and smoke from cigarettes collects in the lungs of a smoker, making them dirty and blocking the tiny **alveoli.** This leads to a general decrease in the ability of the lungs to work efficiently. Cigarette smoke has three main components: tar, carbon monoxide, and nicotine. Each damages the body in some way:

- *Tar:* This irritates the lining of the airways, destroying the **cilia** that usually sweep out dust and **microorganisms. Mucus** builds up, leading to infection and inflammation, and a "smoker's cough" develops as the person repeatedly tries to clear the airways. Eventually, bronchitis and emphysema may develop.
- *Carbon monoxide:* This affects the arteries, causing them to harden and narrow. The heart has to work harder to pump blood around the body, so all activities and exercise take more effort, and even small movements can cause breathlessness.
- *Nicotine:* This is a drug, and it is the part of the smoke to which people become addicted. Many people say that smoking helps them to stay calm and relaxed—but it also leads to high blood pressure, clogged blood vessels, and heart disease.

Scientists have shown that the combined effects of the components of cigarette smoke can lead to serious illnesses, such as heart disease, stroke, chronic bronchitis, emphysema, and cancer of the mouth, throat, and lungs.

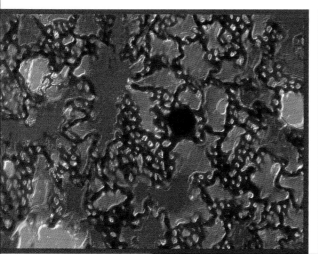 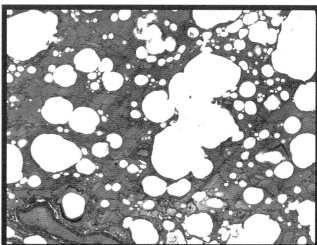

The picture on the left shows a section from a normal lung. The picture on the right shows a section from a lung that has been damaged by emphysema. The white areas are the enlarged and damaged alveoli.

Women smokers

Pregnant women who smoke put their babies at risk. Doctors have found that babies born to mothers who smoked while pregnant are smaller, lighter, and weaker than babies of nonsmokers. Babies of smoking mothers have also been shown to have an increased risk of heart and breathing problems.

Smoking can have other unpleasant side effects too, including:
* wrinkles near the eyes and mouth, speeding up aging of the skin
* yellowed hair and fingers
* brown, stained teeth
* bad breath
* varicose veins.

Secondhand smoke

Secondhand smoke is another serious problem. If a person in a room is smoking, the cigarette smoke does not just stay close to him or her—it drifts around the room, mixing with the rest of the air. Anybody else in the room will have to breathe in the cigarette smoke, too. This can lead to serious health problems, even for nonsmokers. Smoking is now banned in many public places, such as offices, shops, hospitals, and most buses and trains. In many companies, workers are allowed to smoke only outside the building.

If cigarette smoke collects in a room, as in this picture, even the nonsmokers have to **inhale** it. If parents continue to smoke around their children, they are putting them

Giving up smoking

Smoking is linked to some dangerous diseases. Scientists and doctors generally agree that smokers are not likely to live as long as nonsmokers are. Smokers are also more likely to be disabled by smoking-related diseases. To make people aware of the damage they may be doing to themselves by smoking, many countries now have laws requiring a health warning to be printed on every pack of cigarettes.

There are a variety of things available to help people to stop smoking, such as nicotine gum, nicotine patches, and "dummy," or fake, cigarettes. Doctors can also prescribe some drugs for people who need extra help to give up smoking.

BREATHING MECHANICS

Lungs cannot draw air into themselves—they need to be blown up and then deflated, much like blowing air into a balloon and then letting the air rush out of it. **Inhaling** and **exhaling** require the coordinated contraction and relaxation of the **diaphragm** and other muscles in the rib cage and abdomen.

Inhalation

Inhalation is an active event—muscles have to contract to make it happen.

- The diaphragm contracts, making itself flatter, and it moves downward away from the chest space.
- The **intercostal** muscles between the ribs contract, moving the rib cage and **sternum** upward and outward.

These two actions make the chest space larger, so the air pressure (the force of air pushing on the airways) inside the chest is lower than the air pressure outside. Air is drawn into the lungs until the pressure inside equals the pressure outside.

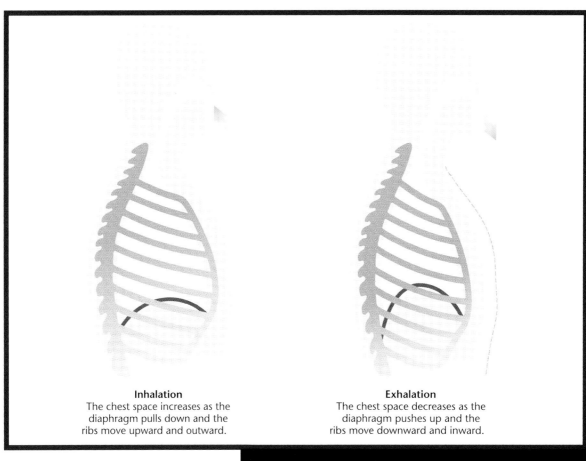

Inhalation
The chest space increases as the diaphragm pulls down and the ribs move upward and outward.

Exhalation
The chest space decreases as the diaphragm pushes up and the ribs move downward and inward.

These diagrams show how the movements of the ribs and diaphragm are important in breathing.

Exhalation

Exhalation is a passive event—it happens naturally as muscles relax back to their resting positions, like an elastic band springing back after it has been stretched.
- The diaphragm relaxes. It becomes more dome-shaped and pushes upward toward the chest space.
- The intercostal muscles relax, allowing the ribs and sternum to move downward and inward.

These muscle relaxations make the chest space smaller, so the air pressure inside the chest is higher than the air pressure outside. Air is forced out of the chest, until the pressures inside and outside are equal.

Lying down

Have you ever wondered why patients in hospitals are propped up on their pillows? If you lie flat on your back, gravity causes the abdominal organs to push against the diaphragm. This makes it harder for the diaphragm to contract, so inhalation is difficult.

Although we usually sleep lying flat, our respiratory systems would function more easily if we propped ourselves up a little. Raising the head and shoulders into a half-sitting position means that gravity pulls the abdominal organs down, away from the diaphragm. It also pulls on the diaphragm itself, so inhalation becomes easier.

Controlling breathing

Singers and wind instrument players need to control their breathing so that they can release air exactly how and when they wish. They are trained to relax their abdominal muscles when they inhale, gradually contracting them as they exhale to control the outflow of air.

BREATHING CONTROL

We can control our breathing for a short while, but we usually breathe without thinking about it, whether we are awake or asleep, active or resting. Breathing is controlled by involuntary signals from the brain, and these in turn are regulated by feedback from the rest of the body. The respiratory center in the brain controls the contraction of the muscles involved in breathing. It is situated in the **brain stem,** in areas called the medulla oblongata and the pons.

With training and practice, people can exert a lot of control over their breathing. This is necessary in order to play instruments such as a trumpet.

In normal breathing, **inhalation** lasts for just under two seconds, and **exhalation** for just under three seconds. The respiratory center has two separate circuits of nerve cells that work alternately. One circuit, the I circuit, triggers inhalation, and the other, the E circuit, triggers exhalation.

Fast and slow

Sometimes, we need to breathe more quickly or more slowly, so it is important that the respiratory center responds to what is happening in the rest of the body:

- *Carbon dioxide concentration:* If the level of carbon dioxide in the blood begins to increase, the respiratory center will speed up the breathing rate to get more oxygen.
- *Exercise:* When we exercise, signals from sensors in joints and muscles are relayed to the respiratory center, and the breathing rate is increased to keep up with the body's movement.
- *Lungs:* Stretch receptors in the lungs send signals to the respiratory center, giving information about how much the lungs are stretched.

We can consciously stop or change our breathing pattern for a short time, because the cerebral cortex (the part of the brain that deals with our thoughts) can override the respiratory center. However, as soon as the carbon dioxide levels in the blood begin to rise, the respiratory center takes control again, and normal breathing resumes whether we want it to or not!

Swimming and diving

Control of breathing is very important for swimmers and divers. Swimmers need to match their breathing with their strokes. For example, in the breaststroke, the head lifts as the hands push backward, making it easy to take a breath—but when the hands push forward, the head dips underwater and it is impossible to take a breath. Divers need to take in a large breath before they hit the water, so that they have enough air to last until they surface and can breathe again.

Most of the time, there is plenty of air around us for most people to breathe normally. However, sometimes people go into situations where there is little or no air, so they need to have their own air supplies with them.

Underwater divers

Swimming just below the surface of the water is possible using a snorkel. Its short, hollow pipe allows you to breathe without having to come to the surface. To dive deeper, a supply of air is needed. Divers who are not going to great depths carry tanks of compressed air (air at a higher pressure than in the atmosphere) strapped to their backs, and breathe through a mouthpiece connected to the tank by a hose. For diving to greater depths, other mixtures of gases may be used. Nitrox, a mixture of nitrogen and oxygen, has more oxygen and less nitrogen than normal air. Some divers use a mixture of helium and oxygen without any nitrogen, and some use a mixture of all three gases.

Decompression sickness

The deeper a diver goes, the greater the pressure of the water on his or her body. As the pressure increases, so does the amount of nitrogen that can dissolve in the liquid of the blood. This does not cause a problem until the diver wants to return to the surface. If the diver

Humans cannot breathe underwater, so divers need to take their own air supplies.

comes up too quickly, the pressure decreases too suddenly, and the nitrogen dissolved in the blood comes out of solution as bubbles of gas. The bubbles are carried around the body in the blood and may lodge in tissues near the joints, causing a lot of pain. This is called decompression sickness, or "the bends," and it can be fatal. Divers avoid it by coming up very slowly so that the nitrogen diffuses out of the blood without forming bubbles.

Firefighters

Firefighters need to use special breathing devices to enter smoke-filled buildings. There is plenty of air in the buildings, but the smoke mixed with the air would choke the firefighters very quickly. In industrial fires and explosions, dangerous chemicals may be released into the air, so firefighters need a way to supply air that is safe to breathe. Cylinders of compressed air are strapped to their backs. Modern breathing devices have built-in communications systems and personal alarms.

Astronauts

There is no atmosphere in space, so astronauts must carry their own oxygen supplies if they leave the safe environment of a space center or shuttle. They use a PLSS (Primary Life Support System) with a backpack that supplies oxygen, maintains the air pressure and temperature, and absorbs moisture and carbon dioxide. Their spacesuits are maintained at a lower pressure than that inside the space shuttle, so they have a different problem from deep sea divers—if they go straight out, they will suffer from decompression sickness as nitrogen bubbles out of their blood. They have to spend several hours breathing pure oxygen before they step out into space. This removes any nitrogen that is dissolved in their body fluids and keeps bubbles from forming when the pressure is suddenly reduced. NASA is trying to reduce this problem by developing new spacesuits that will maintain a higher pressure.

The effects of altitude

As you climb higher and higher, the amount of oxygen in the atmosphere decreases. People from lower areas who visit areas of high altitude may suffer from altitude sickness—the lack of oxygen makes them feel tired, dizzy, faint, and sick. People who live in high altitudes all the time are able to breathe normally because their bodies have adapted to the lack of oxygen by producing extra red blood cells. This also means that athletes from those high areas are sometimes able to achieve outstanding performances at lower altitudes. Mountaineers who attempt to climb very high peaks can avoid altitude sickness by climbing to one level and then resting for a few days, giving their bodies time to get used to the lack of oxygen before climbing any higher.

We need to breathe to stay alive, so anything that interrupts the breathing process is potentially very serious. Some problems can be dealt with easily, while others may require specialized treatment.

Choking

It is quite common to choke on a piece of food. Usually, this can be dislodged by coughing. However, if that does not work, a person trained in first aid can use the Heimlich maneuver to force the food out. If this procedure is not carried out properly, the liver, ribs, and lungs may be damaged—so leave it to the experts!

Anaphylactic shock

Anaphylactic shock is the result of an **allergic reaction.** Most allergies may simply cause a rash or an itch, but sometimes a person's body may react very swiftly when exposed to something that triggers his or her allergies—such as peanuts or a wasp sting. The airways get narrower, restricting the flow of air and causing wheeziness. This condition must be treated quickly, using an injection of epinephrine to reverse the effects and open the airways. People likely to suffer from this often carry their epinephrine in an **epi-pen**.

Suffocation

A person suffocates if he or she does not get enough oxygen. This can be as a result of:

- *strangulation*—something compresses the throat, preventing the flow of air into and out of the lungs
- *drowning*—water is breathed into the lungs, affecting their ability to process oxygen
- *choking*—a foreign object blocks the airways
- *blockage*—the nose and mouth are blocked, keeping air from entering
- *gases*—breathing in carbon monoxide keeps the blood from transporting oxygen.

All of these situations prevent air from getting to the lungs, causing the body to become starved for oxygen. Our brains cannot work without oxygen, so death follows within minutes.

First aid

Knowing how to help someone who is in difficulty can be very useful. Why not find out more about first aid? You could get a book from a library, look for information on the Internet, or join an organization such as the Red Cross.

Artificial resuscitation

If a person has stopped breathing, it is important to get oxygen into his or her body. Although the air we **exhale** contains less oxygen than the air around us, there is still enough oxygen in it to keep a person alive. Trained rescuers can use their own breath to help a patient who has stopped breathing. The rescuer must first check the airway for any blockage that may be preventing breathing. Then he or she positions the body to open the airway and breathes into the person's mouth. After checking to see if the chest has risen, the rescuer may give more breaths if necessary. Although artificial respiration is easily learned, it is important to get proper training before carrying it out.

If a person's heart has stopped beating too, **CPR (cardiopulmonary resuscitation)** may be needed. This involves giving chest compressions to stimulate circulation. These methods are simple but can save lives. Many organizations, such as the Red Cross, offer courses to train ordinary people to carry them out.

These medical students are using special dummies to practice giving mouth-to-mouth resuscitation.

WHAT CAN GO WRONG WITH MY LUNGS?

This book has explained the different parts of the lungs and airways, telling why they are important and how they can be damaged by injury and illness. These pages summarize some of the problems that can affect young people. The table also gives you information about how each problem is treated.

Many problems can also be avoided by good health behavior. This is called prevention. Exercising regularly and getting plenty of rest are important, as is eating a balanced diet. This is especially true in your teenage years, when your body is still developing. The table tells you some of the ways you can prevent injury and illness.

Remember, if you think something is wrong with your body, you should always talk to a trained medical professional, like a doctor or a school nurse. Regular medical checkups are an important part of maintaining a healthy body.

Illness	Cause	Symptoms	Prevention	Treatment
Asthma	**Allergens**; hot or cold air; exercise; emotional upset.	Coughing; wheezing; breathlessness.	Reduce stress; use inhalers; avoid triggers.	Use inhaled medicine.
Bronchitis	Exposure to smoke, allergens, and other pollutants.	Chronic cough; wheezing; shortness of breath.	Avoid exposure to pollutants, allergens, and smoke.	Do breathing exercises; pure oxygen therapy can help also.
Carbon monoxide poisoning	Inhaling too much carbon monoxide.	Difficulty breathing; feeling dizzy or sleepy.	Avoid gas and smoke in closed areas; use detectors.	Breathe pure oxygen to restore the body's supply.
Laryngitis	Infection; exposure to cigarette smoke; shouting.	Sore throat; hoarse voice; inability to speak.	Avoid cigarette smoke; do not strain voice.	Rest voice completely; **inhale** warm steam.

Illness	Cause	Symptoms	Prevention	Treatment
Pharyngitis	Bacterial or viral infection; chronic cases caused by too much alcohol or smoking.	Sore throat; swelling in neck.	Avoid smoking or drinking too much alcohol.	Suck on throat lozenges; drink warm liquids; take **antibiotics** for a bacterial infection.
Pleurisy	Infection of **pleural membranes.**	Intense pain accompanied by scratchy, grating breathing.	Maintain good general health with regular exercise and a balanced diet.	Take antibiotics or painkillers; drain excess fluid out of the chest in severe cases.
Pneumonia	Inflammation of the lungs from bacterial infection.	Fever; chills; cough; chest pain; tiredness.	Maintain good general health with regular exercise and a balanced diet.	Take antibiotics; use other drugs to clear airways; use chest **physiotherapy.**
Tonsillitis	Usually bacterial infection of the tonsils.	Sore throat; difficulty with swallowing; sometimes an earache and a stiff neck.	Practice good oral hygiene; maintain good general health by eating a balanced diet.	Drink warm liquids; eat soft foods; use throat lozenges, antibiotics, or painkillers; remove tonsils in severe cases.

Further Reading

Cohen, Joel H. *Tuberculosis.* Farmington Hills, Mich.: Gale Group, 2002.

Connolly, Sean. *Tobacco.* Chicago: Heinemann Library, 2000.

Hayhurst, Chris. *The Lungs: Learning How We Breathe.* New York: The Rosen Publishing Group, Inc., 2001.

Lee, Justin. *The Respiratory System.* New York: The Rosen Publishing Group, Inc., 2000.

Walker, Pam, and Elaine Wood. *The Respiratory System.* Farmington Hills, Mich.: Gale Group, 2002.

GLOSSARY

aerobic respiration process using oxygen to release energy from glucose

allergic reaction way the body responds when exposed to something it is sensitive to, such as the runny nose and sore eyes of hay fever sufferers when exposed to pollens

allergy sensitivity to a particular substance that may lead to an allergic reaction

alveolus (plural is **alveoli**) tiny air sac of the lung

anaerobic respiration process releasing energy from glucose without using oxygen

antibiotic drug used to destroy harmful bacteria and fungi

bacterium (plural is **bacteria**) microorganism that can cause infection

brain stem part of the brain that relays messages between the brain and the spinal cord

bronchiole narrow airway formed by the branching of a bronchus

bronchus (plural is **bronchi**) one of the main airways formed by the branching of the trachea

carbohydrate nutrient that can be broken down to release energy

capillary very fine blood vessel that links arteries to veins

cartilage strong, flexible material that protects bones

chemical reaction change that causes one or more substances to turn into different substances

cilium (plural is **cilia**) microscopic hair on the surface of some airways

CPR (cardiopulmonary resuscitation) method that may be used in an emergency to help a person who has stopped breathing and whose heart has stopped beating

decongestant drug that may be taken to reduce the amount of mucus in the airways

deoxygenated having had the oxygen removed

diaphragm strong sheet of muscle that forms the bottom of the chest space

epi-pen small container with a sterile needle attached that allows immediate administration of epinephrine by injection into a muscle, usually the thigh

exhale to breathe out

exothermic giving off heat

hemoglobin compound found in red blood cells that transports oxygen around the body

hormone chemical made in the body that travels around the body and affects organs and tissues in a variety of ways

influenza type of viral infection

inhale to breathe in

intercostal between the ribs

lung capacity maximum amount of air that can be held in the lungs

membrane thin covering layer of tissue

microorganism tiny living thing that can be seen only under a microscope

molecule smallest unit or particle of a substance made of two or more joined atoms

mucus sticky, slimy fluid that provides lubrication in the body

nasal cavity space inside the skull at the top of the nose

oxygenated having had oxygen added

physiotherapy treatment of disease or injury by massage and movement

pleural membrane membrane surrounding the lungs

protein type of large molecule that makes up some of the basic structures of all living things

pulmonary having to do with the lungs

sensory having to do with the senses

sinus hollow space inside a cranial or facial bone

sternum breastbone

steroid one of a class of drugs that may be used for a variety of reasons, including reduction of inflammation

vertebra (plural is **vertebrae**) one of the bones of the spine

virus very small microorganism that can cause infection